Earth and Space

John Stringer

Contents

Home in the stars

This is a galaxy – a gigantic star city made up of billions of stars.
There are millions of galaxies in space, but this is the one we live in. It's called the Milky Way.

What are stars?

Stars aren't solid like the ground. They are made of gases like the air around you. The gases burn and this makes the stars very hot and very bright.

You can sometimes see patterns of stars at night.

The Sun

What is the Sun?

The Sun is really a star. It's just one of the millions of stars in the Milky Way. Like all stars, it's a huge ball of super-hot gas. We call it our Sun because it's the star we travel round. It's at the heart of our solar system.

4

What is the solar system?

We live on planet Earth. Our planet has eight neighbours. Together, these nine planets all travel around the Sun. These planets and their moons are called the solar system.

The solar system: Sun, Mercury, Venus, Earth, Mars, Jupiter, Saturn, Uranus, Neptune, Pluto

Our light and warmth

Planet Earth is about 150 million kilometres from the Sun. Here, the Earth gets just the right amount of heat. It also gets light. Without light and warmth, there would be no life on Earth.

Where is the Sun at night?

Even during the night the Sun is shining brightly out in space.

The Earth spins completely once every day. At night your part of the Earth is facing away from the Sun – so you can't see it. When it moves back round into the Sun's light, we call it day.

Earth: a spinning ball

You, and everyone you know, live on a huge ball of rock that is spinning in space. The ball is your home – planet Earth.

Why don't you fall off?

You can't fall off the Earth because something is holding you down. There is an invisible force pulling down called gravity. It keeps you on the ground every moment of the day. Gravity pulls on everything. When you drop an egg, it falls to the floor because gravity is pulling it down to the Earth.

Water for life

The Earth looks blue from space. This is because most of the planet is covered by water.

Where is all the water?

Oceans and seas cover nearly three-quarters of the Earth. There are also lakes and rivers, ponds and puddles. Clouds are made of water, too.

Is water important?

Water is very important. In fact, nothing can live without it. None of the other planets in our solar system has running water, and none of them has life.

11

The changing seasons

In many places, warm summers change
into cold winters. They change slowly but
surely as the Earth moves round the Sun.
The journey around the Sun takes one year.
The Earth is slightly tilted. When the top
half of the Earth is tilted towards the Sun,
it has summer. But at the same time the
bottom half of the Earth has winter.

All change

As the Earth moves on round the Sun, the bottom half moves nearer the Sun. Summer arrives here, while the top half of the Earth begins to shiver.

Summer

Autumn

Winter

Spring

The Moon and moonlight

A moon is a rocky ball that travels round a planet. The Earth's Moon moves in a circle, with the same side always pointing towards us.

What is moonlight?

The Moon has no light of its own. What we call moonlight is really sunlight. The sunlight is bounced down to us from the Moon.

The Moon changes

Earth from
the Moon

The changing Moon

To our eyes, the Moon seems to grow bigger
and smaller. It doesn't really. We can only see
the light part of the Moon. The rest is in
shadow. As the Moon moves round the Earth,
the shadow changes shape.

15

A dry world

The Moon is the Earth's nearest neighbour. Astronauts have walked on it. Scientists have examined rocks from it.

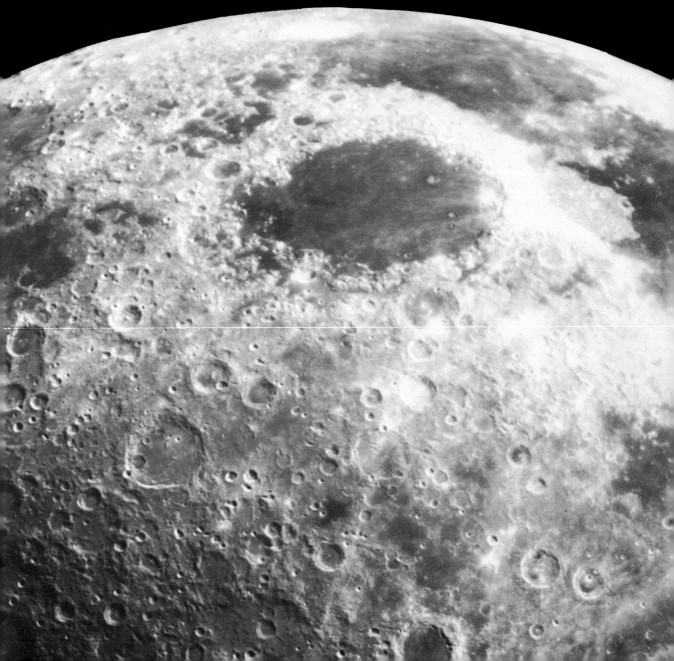

The Moon is dry. There is no air to breathe or water to drink. No plants or animals have ever lived there. The Moon has no weather. It doesn't rain or snow. There's no wind or fog. The days are scorching, but at night it's freezing. Nothing ever changes there. A footprint in the dust will last for ever.

17

Nearest to the Sun

Mercury

Mercury is a small planet, the nearest to the Sun.
On Mercury, days are very long. It gets so hot that
if a spaceship landed, it would melt in the heat!

18 Yet during the long nights it is bitterly cold

Venus

You can sometimes see Venus shining in the night sky. For a better view, space probes have sent back pictures to Earth. They show thick clouds of poisonous gas. The blanket of clouds makes Venus the hottest planet in the solar system.

An artist's view of Venus

Mars: the red planet

Mars is called the red planet because it has red, rusty rocks. Strong winds blow red sand across its rocky surface.

Cold as ice

Mars is the next planet after Earth from the Sun. It is smaller and colder than Earth. All its water is frozen into ice caps.

An artist's view of ancient Mars

Was there life on Mars?

Long ago, Mars may have been warmer. There may have been running water instead of solid ice. We know that living things need warmth and water, but space probes have visited Mars, and they didn't find any signs of life.

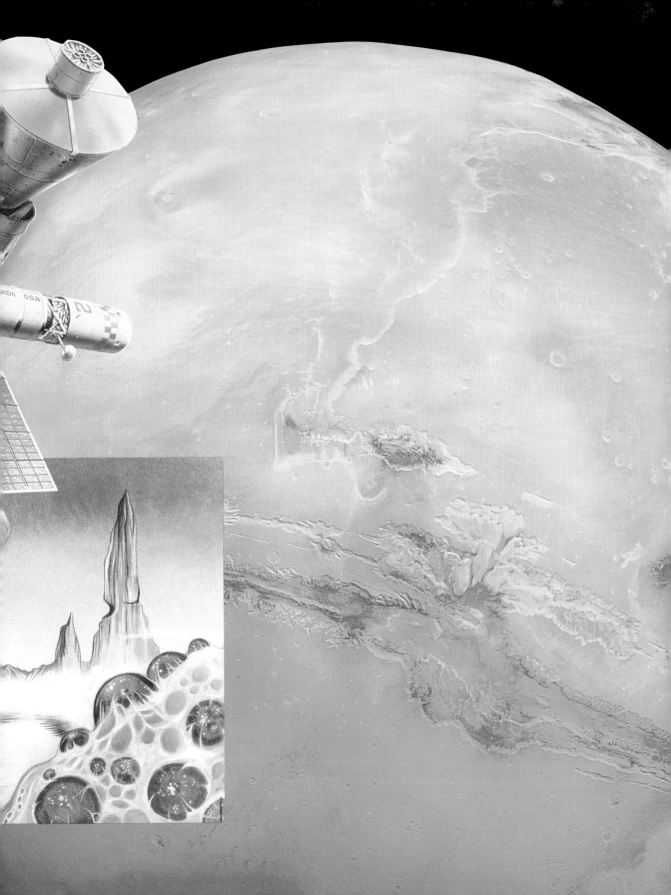

The giant planets

Jupiter and Saturn are the largest planets in the solar system.

Jupiter

Jupiter is not a solid, rocky planet like Earth. Instead it's made of heavy gas. Clouds of gas swirl round the planet in strong winds. Jupiter has at least 16 moons, three of them are big, but the rest are very small.

Saturn

Saturn's shining rings make it the most beautiful planet in the solar system. The rings look solid but are made of millions of pieces of rock and ice.

Saturn's rings

Faraway worlds

Uranus, Neptune and Pluto lie on the edge of our solar system – far from the Sun's warmth.

Uranus and Neptune

Uranus and Neptune are about the same size, and they both have rings around them. Clouds of gas swirl around them. The clouds give them a blue-green colour.

Uranus

Pluto

Neptune

24

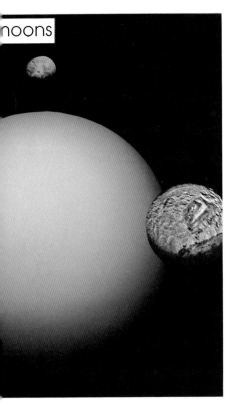

moons

Neptune

Pluto

Pluto is a very tiny, freezing planet – the furthest planet from the Sun. Its journey round the Sun has a different shape from the other planets, and it sometimes curves between Neptune and Uranus.

Shooting stars, comets and meteorites

Shooting stars, comets and meteorites are all parts of the solar system.

What are shooting stars?
On a clear night you may see shooting stars dart across the sky and disappear. They are specks of dust burning up in space.

What are comets?
Comets travel round the Sun. They are made of dust and ice, and have a bright head and tail. Scientists watch them as they travel past the Earth.

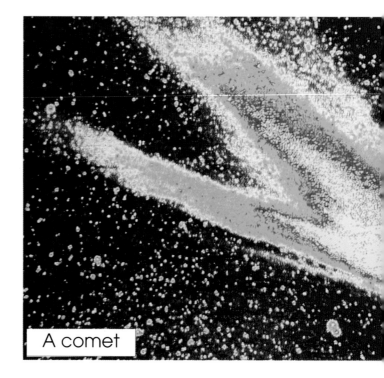

A comet

A falling meteorite

What are meteorites?

Meteorites are chunks of space rock that crash to Earth. When a meteorite fell on Arizona, USA, it left a crater over a kilometre wide!

A meteorite

27

Satellites and probes

Satellites and space probes travel in space. They send back photographs and signals to the Earth.

What do satellites do?

Satellites travel round the Earth. Some satellites take useful photos of the land and sea; some tell us more about the weather; and others send radio and television signals. Some satellites are used to spy on other countries.

What are space probes?

Space probes travel through the solar system. Some probes visit other planets. Others pass close by, and send back wonderful pictures to scientists on Earth.

People in space

The first person to go into space was Yuri Gagarin in 1961. Eight years later, Neil Armstrong walked on the Moon. Since then many people – both men and women – have travelled in space.

What do astronauts do?

Astronauts work in space. They do experiments, launch and repair satellites, and take photographs.

Spacecraft

Most spacecraft can make
only one flight into space.
But a space shuttle can fly
again and again – thanks to
huge booster rockets. The
rockets launch the shuttle
into space, and then fall
back to Earth.

Index

HarperCollins Children's Books

A Division of HarperCollins Publishers Ltd, 77–85 Fulham Palace Road, Hammersmith, London W6 8JB

First published 1994 in the United Kingdom

Reprinted 1996

Copyright © HarperCollins*Publishers* 1994

ISBN 0 00 196542 5

A CIP record is available from the British Library

Illustrated by David Marshall. Photographs: Glen Alison/TSW (13), Julian Baum/SPL (28/29),R Cannon/Life File (11), P Chesley/TSW (10), Dalton/Quadrant (13), Ducros/Jerrican/SPL (28/29), ESA/PLI/SPL (8/9), Fred Espenak/SPL (2/3, 26/7), Coo Science Features (13), David A Hardy/SPL (20/21), Hideo Kurihara/TSW (6), Martin Marrietta Corp./SPL (28/29), NASA/SPL (4/5, 14/15, 16/17, 22/23, 24/25, 26/27, 30/31), NASA/SPL coloured by Mehau Kulyk (18/19), Pekka Parviainen/SPL (26/27), John Sanford/SPL (14/15), Stephen Studd/TSW (13), Nicola Sutton/Life File (9), Tony Stone Worldwide (6, 10, 13), US Geological Survey/SPL (20/21).

Prepared by *specialist publishing services* 090 857 307; Series editor: Nick Hutchins; Editor: Claire Llewellyn; Design: Eric Drewery/Susi Martin; Picture research: Lorraine Sennett

Printed and bound in Hong Kong